Praying the Psalms

Also by J. Barrie Shepherd

Diary of Daily Prayer

*A Diary of Prayer: Daily Meditations
on the Parables of Jesus*

*Encounters: Poetic Meditations
on the Old Testament*

Prayers from the Mount

Praying
the
Psalms

Daily Meditations
on Cherished Psalms

J. Barrie Shepherd

WP

The Westminster Press
Philadelphia

Book design by Christine Schueler

First edition

Published by The Westminster Press®
Philadelphia, Pennsylvania

PRINTED IN THE UNITED STATES OF AMERICA
9 8 7 6 5 4 3 2 1

Library of Congress Cataloging-in-Publication Data

Shepherd, J. Barrie.
    Praying the Psalms.

    1. Bible. O.T. Psalms—Meditations.   2. Devotional
calendars.   I. Title.
BS1430.4.S53 1987   242'.2   87–8156
ISBN 0–664–24070–4 (pbk.)

I dedicate this book
in gratitude to God for the life of
J. ERNEST SOMERVILLE
prince of the pulpit and friend

"For auld lang syne, my dear . . ."

Contents

Preface

As with my previous books presented in this "prayer diary" format, space has been made available between the prayers for each day so that the reader/prayer can claim this book for his or her own. It is my hope that this will also become your diary and that my prayers will spark creations of your own—notes, poems, meditations—which may chart for you your personal pilgrimage through this most ancient prayer book, the book of Psalms.

It should go without saying that the particular psalm chosen for each day should be read thoroughly and meditatively before launching into the suggested prayers. If possible I would suggest that each psalm be read aloud. After all, they were originally intended to be heard within the context of worship, not read from any printed page. Indeed, an alternative title for this book might well be "Songs of the Spirit," for these psalms are poetry, not prose. They cry out to be sung, to be chorused, to be chanted, to be lamented—to be anything but read, as they too often are, like the closing prices on the New York Stock Exchange.

As far as language about God is concerned, I have tended to stick fairly close to that found within the psalter. Where the psalmist employs feminine images about God, as in Psalm 131, I have followed suit; but, on the whole, I have stuck with the more traditional terms, "Father," "Lord," and "God." To any whom this might offend I offer my sincere apologies, hoping that the prayers themselves will overcome such shortcomings and speak directly from the soul to God by whatever name the prayer/reader chooses to employ.

This book marks for me the completion of twenty-one years of ordained ministry. Over the years I have been continually encouraged by the friendly responses I have received to these little books and other writings of mine. I thank God for whatever gifts have been entrusted to me and for whatever help they may have brought to pilgrims like myself.

Swarthmore, Pennsylvania
All Hallows' Eve, 1986

Praying the Psalms

DAY ONE

The Psalms

MORNING

I felt I ought to read the psalms, Lord.
People said they were so wonderful.
All the great saints and theologians
had been formed under their influence,
guided by their insights, deepened through
the rich wisdom of their profundity.
As a newly ordained preacher,
as one who sought to live the Christian life
and grow in it, I felt I ought to read the psalms.

Therefore, as a daily discipline,
a kind of energetic exercise in prayer,
I began to "do" a psalm a day as part
of my devotions. I didn't find it easy.
There seemed to be so much in there of vengeance
and recrimination. The writers of these psalms
spent half their time at least—or so it
seemed to me—in calling down the wrath of God
on others, principally their enemies.
And what a bloodthirsty lot they were,
speaking hopefully of dashing babies' brains
against the rock and other gruesome forms
of retribution! This was not exactly
the kind of Christian charity I had learned
about in Sunday school. There was nothing here
of "turn the other cheek."

So I gave up on the psalms,
couldn't stomach all their bitterness and pain.
Twenty years ago and more that was, and yet, somehow,
I kept on coming back. Perhaps it was the psalms
that just refused to close the book on me.
Anyway, I wrestle with them still, just as you
wrestle with my bitterness and pain, just as
I pray, this day, you wrestle with my life
to shape its broken, twisted forms
into a song.

   Amen.

EVENING

It's not as if the hatred,
the vindictiveness of so many
of these psalms is any more acceptable
to me now, Father, than it was when I first
read them. There are passages among them that
still fill me with disgust, still shock me
with the violence and vitriol they pour out.
It's just that, as the years have come and gone,
I have learned to recognize myself much more,
have tasted for myself the gall of enmity
and anger, have sensed within me
something of the passion that compelled
these all-too-human individuals to write.

You have taught me that the psalms
are as much about myself as about you, Lord.
It has dawned upon me that this towering book
is the one place in these scriptures where we see,
most clearly, not just your Word but our response
in both its glory and its gore. This Psalter
is our half of the equation, the prayer book
of your people, Lord, the record of our human word
in dialogue with eternity.
It is only proper, therefore,
that these psalms reflect, at times,
the anger, hurt, despair, and, yes, the spite,
the vengefulness and rancor of such ordinary folk
as I know myself to be, even when caught up into
the extraordinary moment of encounter with
the living God. Indeed, if they did *not*
do so then I would feel left out.

These days I read the psalms because I see myself,
my strengths, my weaknesses, my victories,
and also my defeats, my all-too-human faults
that are even yet forgiven and redeemed
in Christ my Lord. And so I thank you for the psalms
and seek your blessing for this night.
                                        Amen.

DAY TWO

Psalm 1

MORNING

A signpost, Lord,
that's how this psalm appears to me,
a signpost set up right here at the outset
of this entire book to point out to the reader
two distinct and separate ways: the way of the righteous
and the way of the wicked. It is as if I am being warned
that reading any further will require of me a choice,
a choice between the narrow way to life that Jesus spoke of
and the broad and easy path down to destruction.

This psalm paints that broad and easy way
so insightfully. It speaks at first of walking,
walking "in the counsel of the wicked."
That is when a person just begins to listen, to overhear,
then lets the mind linger for a moment upon the suggestions
of the "easy livers": "Oh, it really doesn't matter."
"Everybody does it, after all." "We're living
in a modern age, man" (as Eve might have said
to Adam), "wise up and don't be so uptight."

Then comes the standing "in the way of sinners."
The footsteps slow a little, the pace slackens, the ear
strains back, head turns, walk comes to a shambling stop,
and instantly one is surrounded by a crowd
with welcome open arms, a crowd who feel somehow

affirmed to have another join their dubious
yet defensive crew. And this is known as
standing in the way of sinners.

Last comes the sitting "in the seat of scoffers"
as one settles in, relinquishes, with some relief,
the long and testing pilgrimage toward meaning, hope,
integrity, and love, and takes a chair along the edge
from which to scoff at and make fun of all those fools
who still persist in seeking God.

Yes, Father, this is a wonderfully subtle,
psychological depiction of the slippery slope
that leads down to the pit. Deliver me, I pray,
this day and all my days from such foolishness as this,
through him whose signpost showed the way that leads
across all other ways to you.
                              Amen.

EVENING

The other way I see here
is the life of faith, Lord God.
The psalmist sees it like a tree
deep-rooted by a river, bearing good fruit,
its leaves gladdening the eye and heart of all
who pass it by, and never withering away.

My faith is not like that, Lord.
Too often, as you well know, it is
a matter of the head, not of the heart,
an intellectual acknowledgment that you do exist
and on some distant throne somewhere
are probably working out, right now,
your purpose for the universe.

I look on faith as "things to be believed in":
the Apostles' Creed, perhaps the Catechism,
or just last Sunday's sermon.
I "believe" all this because it is a comforting idea
to tuck away for use when life turns sour
and I need the consolation.

This ancient writer tells me, God,
that faith can be no passive thing,
no celestial Santa Claus to haul out once a year
and cheer a dismal winter, no mere acceptance
of a set of doctrines, some theory about the origins
of life or the creation of the universe.
Faith involves action, choice, commitment.
It is like setting out upon a journey,
putting one foot before the other on the road
you show to me and trusting you to guide the way I go,
to lead me to the final destination even though
I cannot see beyond one step ahead.

Renew this trust in me during these sleeping hours.
So may I rise refreshed, renewed and eager
for the next stage in my journeying.
                              Amen.

DAY THREE

Psalm 1

MORNING

We don't hear much
in our mainstream churches, Lord,
about judgment nowadays. There was a time
when all religion used to talk about was judgment—
who was going to pass it and who wasn't—
and certainly these psalms do not neglect the theme.
So even here, right at the beginning of the book, I read,
"Therefore the wicked will not stand in the judgment."

I wonder what this psalmist means
when he says "judgment," Father. Does he intend
to conjure up that whole familiar last scenario
of books of life and thrones, the sheep and goats,
eternal bliss, eternal damnation? I don't think so.
Even Jesus, after all, when he spoke about those sheep
and goats was painting a parable, not delivering
a literal, blow-by-blow description.
Yet something in me knows there is a judgment somehow,
somewhere. Oh, it doesn't always seem to work out right.
The innocent do suffer. The sleazy crooked types often
do appear to get away with things.
And yet, looking at things overall, we get back
what we put into life. Live for ourselves and we are
left to ourselves. Live by cheating, lies, and treachery
and, soon or late, we will know betrayal, fear, and loneliness.

We make our own judgment, much of the time,
even, maybe, for all eternity. For if we live a life
of total cynicism, lack of trust, all out for self,
what would we be doing in your presence, Lord?
Would not that be, in itself, a kind of hell,
perhaps even more fearful than any flames
or lake of everlasting fire?

Yes, judgment is a fact of life.
I see it all around me every day. What people sow
they also reap, in one way or another.
One thing I'm thankful for, Lord God,
that in Christ Jesus your justice is ever tempered
by your mercy and your bright amazing grace.

Amen.

EVENING

The Bible scholars, Father,
as I read them in their commentaries,
describe this psalm in many different ways.
But all of them seem so purposeful, so grim.
They define the basic theme as being "duty,"
"obedience," "the law," "the straight and narrow way."
And they all completely miss the point. Not one of them
seems to have read the very first word of this old psalm,
of this old Psalter.

The word is "blessed": "Blessed is the one,"
"Makarioi" in the Greek just like the Beatitudes,
meaning "joyful," "full of happiness."
"Oh, the wonderful elation of the one who lives
like this." That's what this psalm is really saying
to me here. And it's really a Beatitude, just like the ones
that Jesus spoke. This psalm, this entire Psalter
begins in joy and exultation.

Again, I look a little farther and I read,
"But his delight is in the law of the Lord."
Not "his burden," "his obligation," not "his dreary,
drawn-out duty," but "his delight" is in your law.
Why do so many people get just enough religion
to make themselves, and other people, thoroughly miserable,
Father? And never enough to break through to delight?

Lord God, help me to know, above all else,
the *joy* of thy salvation. Teach me,
as the Catechism used to put it, to glorify you
and enjoy you forever, and not to forget to enjoy.
And grant me as I sleep to share the holy merriment
of the angels as they dance around your throne,
as they observe the antics of your creatures here below.
So may I rest in you and rise to greet the light
with fresh delight.
                    Amen.

DAY FOUR

Psalm 2

MORNING

Some of these psalms must have been composed
not in the temple but in the royal palace,
the court of the kings of ancient Israel.
This second psalm seems to breathe that kind of atmosphere,
Lord, with its talk of nations and rulers, conspiracies
and councils. There is an air here of politics,
of international affairs, alliances,
treaties, and the like.

There are many today who would divorce these two,
keep politics and religion completely separate, Lord.
They argue that religion is a matter of the inner,
spiritual life of persons, and that politics is
too partisan, too open to abuse and propaganda,
too divisive on specific issues to have
any place in the religious life.

And yet this psalm and so many others,
so much of this Bible, in fact, is concerned with
questions and concerns that are most certainly political.
They deal with laws and government, with foreign policy
and civil rights. This psalm, for instance,
seems to be proclaiming that you, O Lord,
are on the side of Israel's king.
The text issues a warning to any and all other nations

to get in line, submit themselves to the rule
of your chosen one, your favorite, before it is too late.

It certainly would be nice, Lord,
to feel that you were always on my side,
backing me up in everything I did, working things out
so that I could be your favorite, top dog.
It certainly would be nice, and yet,
that's not the way you have been operating
in my life so far. More often than not it seems
that I'm the one who *gets* the warning rather than
the one who gives it. But something tells me that,
despite all this, in a deeper, more basic sense,
you truly are always on my side.

So walk beside me all throughout this day,
in Jesus Christ I pray.
                    Amen.

EVENING

The deeper message of this second psalm
is not that politics and religion shouldn't mix,
but rather that one must not try to use religion
in order to baptize any cause, concern, or candidate,
no matter how righteous they may seem to be
at that particular moment.

You taught this lesson to the Jews
through many centuries of disappointment
with their "divinely chosen" rulers, Lord.
In one way or another, they all had feet of clay.
Not one of them, not even David, could live up
to the image presented here and elsewhere in the psalms:
"You are my son, today I have begotten you."

And so, out of this failure, you brought forth
the concept of a promised future king, a ruler,
yet to be, who would fulfill these ancient promises.
"Mashiach" was what they called him—the anointed one.
And they looked forward to his coming, still do today
with longing and great hope.

So this second psalm, for all its
petty grasping after power on the surface,
points far beyond itself to one who truly was,
and is, and ever shall be your "begotten son,"
one who will rule with justice and with righteousness,
one who will call, and calls today, the rulers of
the nations, the presidents and premiers,
the generals and the commissars, and cries to them:

> Watch out! Beware! Be warned, O rulers of the earth.
> Serve the Lord with fear, with trembling kiss his feet.

Lord, rule my life this night,
let me sleep under your governance.
So may I know the blessing that is promised here
to all those who take refuge in you.
                                        Amen.

DAY FIVE
Psalm 8

MORNING

Father, this question, "Who am I?"
or, rather, "Who are we, we members of this
race called human?" has exercised the mind
since ever you gave us minds to exercise.
The psalmist asks it here in the context of
your grandeur, the created glory of your starry heavens.
And I have asked it too. I have stood alone on mountaintop
or seashore, beneath the dark and velvet vault of heaven,
traced the myriad bright markings of this mystery called Cosmos
and felt exhilarated, ravished by the splendor,
yet, at the same time, somehow lost, insignificant,
beneath its awe-full crushing magnitude.

The paradox of humankind, Lord,
that is what I struggle with as I read this splendid psalm,
as I stand before the wonders of creation.
These hands that clasp before you now in prayer
are hands that carved cathedrals, the radiance
of Chartres, Canterbury, Cologne. They are also hands
that strung the barbed-wire fences, stoked the ovens
of the concentration camps, Dachau, Belsen, Auschwitz.
This mind now grappling with words and images
can devise an artificial heart, splice a human gene,
trace back the forming of this universe to one minute
before zero; can also conjure evils like apartheid,

can even shape devices that may empty out this universe
of life, once and for all. The paradox of humanity.

The psalmist takes this paradox—your paradox created
from the mud, Lord God, and breathed full of your spirit—
and sets it in the context of your majesty
so that the paradox can live, not only live but love,
can even know, by your grace, a little glory of its own
as your creation, Lord, your creature.

In this identity, within
the overarching context of your grandeur
and your grace, I would live out this day in hope,
and in humility.
                    Amen.

EVENING

One further answer has been given
to that age-old question, "What is man?"
This psalm, in all its beauty of expression,
points beyond itself, Lord God, to One who was
to come and to fulfill the dream of humankind
that is found written in the stars.

"Behold the man!" cried Pontius Pilate:
ecce homo, bearing unwitting yet eternal witness,
pointing to the answer you have provided,
Father, for this question of the ages.
"What is man?"—"Behold the man!"

In this to all appearances defeated human life,
in this apparently dejected figure of a prisoner, flogged,
in chains, on the way to execution, you have shown to us
the vision of what human life can be, must be,
if we are ever to achieve the goal you made us for.

That love in which your Son, our Savior,
offered up his life on my behalf; the way in which
he broke the chains of hate and hell, refusing to return
evil for evil, pain for pain, but took into himself
the gathered enmity of all our race, absorbed it
rather than to pass it on to future generations;
the grace with which he lived and died your grace,
making of his death, not a curse, but a gift
to all humanity from that day on—all this
shows us your answer to this question,
"What is man?"

Father, forgive me for the ways
that in this day, now past, I failed to live up
to this highest, grandest definition of my own humanity.
By your rich grace, in him, restore me
through these hours of rest and sleep
so that my walk may hold more closely to the path
that he has set before me, so that my life may find
its meaning and its majesty within the context
of the gospel of your Son.
                         Amen.

DAY SIX
Psalm 19

MORNING

This psalm is all about a message, Lord,
a message you are sending that is no longer
getting through. If only folk would stop, look,
and listen, step aside out of their insane scramble
after all the shoddy trinkets that are dangled,
glistening, before their eyes, and catch, again,
the old-world sounds of geese above the autumn fog,
and feel the sharp, fresh wind across their faces,
the rich soil beneath their feet, between their fingers.
If we, your people, could only do all this, we might
just reconnect with that earliest of ancestors who,
venturing out beyond the mouth of his smoke-darkened cave,
lifted his eyes above to the star-encrusted heavens,
and exclaimed in wordless awe and wonder,
groped toward thoughts of God.

What progress we have made since that cave mouth!
What inconceivable improvements in all the standards
of our living! Yet I sometimes wonder what it all has cost,
what has been lost along the way, how it is that
we no longer hear the eloquent silence
that speaks to us of you, Lord God.

There is, of course, another side to nature;
there are earthquakes, floods, disease, and human suffering.

So the psalmist, in his delineation of your message,
turns from nature to the marvel of the law.
You not only gave a wondrous world to live in, Father,
you have also showed us how to live in it.
You have given us a Book, a set of clear directions,
on how to take our place within this glorious setting.
And this law is not a crushing, heavy burden,
it is a blessing given us to cherish, to uphold
because it upholds us; because it is the framework,
pattern, model of existence in relationship, in community,
in responsibility, and therefore in the only true
and worthwhile—lasting—freedom.

"The starry heavens above me and the moral law within";
open my eyes this day, Lord, to these signposts
set within the world that point me toward you.
Teach me reverence and obedience—and faith,
which is the fullest combination of the two.

                                                    Amen.

EVENING

At the close of the day,
in this time of contemplation,
this psalm speaks to me of prayer and its power.
I began this day, Father, with the majestic revelation
of creation and with the calm and learned dispensation
of the law. Here, at the climax of the nineteenth psalm,
I reach toward the most direct, most searching pathway
to your presence, the close, personal conversation
of the human heart with its Creator and Redeemer.

And what a distance has been traveled
from that first, primeval gasp of awe and wonder
at the cave mouth to the secret, intimate communion
of the believer with the Lord. Oh! one can stand amazed
before the wonders of the world. One can seek to reason
over all the weightier matters of the law.
But the most amazing wonder, Lord my God, is surely this:
that if I truly open up my soul, my life, to you,
you will come in and be with me, dwell with me.

Help me, thus, to be open.
Let me sense your presence, knocking at the door
of my life, waiting to be welcomed and to offer me
the gifts you bear: trust, hope, and love.
You will not force an entry. You will take few of us
by storm, and faith is a tender plant that must be
cultivated, nurtured, tended, practiced on and with,
in daily disciplines of prayer and Bible study.
You will not solve all my problems, take away all fears
and foes. Indeed, if these scriptures are anything
to go by, you may well bring new problems as you lead me
out to issues like world peace and economic justice,
into healing forms of service to the needy and the poor,
into the uncharted challenges and mysteries of love.

Hear me now, O God, as I breathe the old,
beloved prayer that closes this familiar psalm
and claim it, humbly, for my own:

Let the words of my mouth
and the meditation of my heart
be acceptable in thy sight, O Lord,
my rock and my redeemer.

Amen.

DAY SEVEN
Psalm 22

MORNING

I read the opening words
of this passionate cry—.
"My God, my God, why hast thou forsaken me?"—
and I am transported to Good Friday,
stationed somewhere in that awful, awe-filled crowd,
gathered around the foot of Jesus' cross.

Who was it who stood there to hear that cry?
The mockers and the lovers, or so the Gospels
would suggest; those who couldn't care less and those
who cared so much they risked their lives
to be beside their friend, their Lord,
in his time of agony and desolation.

And yet he died for both—
both the scoffers and the faithful ones;
the suffering he bore that made him cry out
with these dreadful words was just as much on behalf
of the one group as the other.

As I stand here, in my imagination,
I like to believe that I am standing with the ones
who sought to share his pain. Yet even if that
were so, I cannot escape my part in all
that happened there, cannot deny the burden that was added
to the weight he bore on my behalf.

Deliver me, Father, from spiritual pride,
from imagining that I am better than I really am.
Help me to recognize my kinship with those mockers
at the cross, to realize how close I am to them,
how far from him who hung there for my sake.

Grant me, this day, an openness to all
my fellow men and women, no eagerness to judge,
but a love for them partaking of that love
with which your Son, my Savior, gave his life
and cried that desolate cry,
"My God, my God, why hast thou forsaken me?"

Amen.

EVENING

I thank you, Father God,
that I have never been in such extremity
that I could pray a prayer like this one.
Its words are full of anguish, almost terror.
Whoever wrote this psalm must, in some way,
have lived it first. The language is too powerful,
too personal, for this prayer to be a product
merely of imagination.

This past summer I visited
the concentration camp at Dachau.
As I read this psalm, scenes from that day
return before my eyes. I view again the watchtowers
and the wire, the whipping posts, the "solitary" cells.
I trudge across that vast, inhuman parade ground
under the blazing sun and populate it, rank on rank,
with shambling, suffering humanity.
I peer again into those gaping ovens,
then read the endless litanies of names,
statistics, numbers, every one of them a life like mine
with hurts and hopes, fears and loves, promises
never claimed, possibilities never realized.

I remember—it was Sunday morning—
how I heard the church bells ringing from beyond
the electrified fences summoning the Christian folk
of Dachau to worship you, Lord God. And it struck me
like a hammerblow: they must have heard them too.
Those wretched scraps of pain and sheer survival,
as they went about their endless labor unto death,
must have heard the bells and maybe even
prayed this selfsame prayer:
"My God, my God, why hast thou forsaken me?"

Lord, remind me now that others suffer
while I worship you in comfort and in peace.
Show me what I can do to end injustice and oppression.
Then let my peace become true peace
when it is peace for all.
                    Amen.

DAY EIGHT
Psalm 23

MORNING

What is it, in these six short verses, Lord,
that makes this the beloved psalm,
that sets it, somehow, closest to the heart
as the most memorized, the most cherished piece
of literature in all of faith?

One thing I notice here is the simplicity.
This is no formal, scholarly treatise about God.
Instead I find, in humble language, even humbler images:
a shepherd, a flock, a river, valley, table, house—
a song from the heart, to the heart of all humanity.
This is a song that sings about the simplest things:
rest and peace, want and sufficiency, goodness
and evil, fear and death, trust and hope.
Yes, the simplest, most eternal things are here.

And there is honesty throughout this song.
It begins beside the quiet waters and green pastures,
but, before the song is ended, I have also faced
the valley of dark shadows; I have journeyed
through that grim ravine called death.

I notice how the person changes at this point,
from speaking of you as "the Lord" to addressing you
as "Thou." So that, right where I need you most,

just when dark shadows start to fall, the way grows
steep and narrow, and I wish I could turn back,
you join me, not in theory but in person,
and I find the reassurance only your own self can bring.

And here is where the honesty of this psalm
is most powerful of all, that it promises no detours,
no easier, alternative routings for those who love the Lord,
no miraculous deliverance from the dark and dread of death.
It holds out one sure promise—that in the end you will
be there; that every step I take, every fear I know,
you know it with me; that in the valley of the shadow
you will grasp my hand and never let it go.

Then take my hand this day, Good Shepherd,
and, whether it be green pastures or the dark ravine,
walk by my side until I reach your house,
the table set, the cup that overflows.
                          Amen.

EVENING

The very first line of this favorite psalm,
"The Lord is my shepherd, I shall not want,"
captures, unforgettably, the essence of its message,
the essence of all faith, the essence of a true and full
relationship with you, Lord God. And that essence
lies in trust, which is another word for confidence,
which is another word for faith.

You teach me, through your Word, that there
are only two approaches to this gift called life
you give me, Father. My instincts lead me, most,
toward the first. I must protect myself, ensure myself,
defend myself against all possible and conceivable danger.
And thus I miss so much of life, experience in the end
a guaranteed defeat, for nothing can defend me from my death.

The other way, the way of trust, is harder to begin.
It calls for openness, vulnerability, for sharing, giving,
loving—which, this way would argue, life is all about.
This second way seems riskier, too, and yet
this psalm would claim the opposite; would say,
does say, The more I trust, the more I will discover
it is the only way that leads to life.

Not that all my questions are then answered.
Not that all my problems, doubts, and perils are removed.
But that, with my questions, in and through my pains
and problems, I will know a presence and a peace,
a rod and staff sufficient for all trials,
a grace so amazing that it spreads a banquet table,
right in the midst of every kind of danger and distress.

This is the kind of trust
that the writer of this psalm holds out
to me across three thousand years this night,
inviting me to join him as he says, in simple honesty,

    The Lord is my shepherd,
    I shall not want.

Amen.

DAY NINE
Psalm 24

MORNING

When I contemplate the wonders of this world,
this creation you have founded on the seas
and established on the floods, my thoughts return
to one particular spot, Father,
a log cabin on an island off the coast of Maine.
What a thrill I felt when first I called it mine;
when, after long and anxious reckonings,
late nights with pad and pencil and eraser—
we really couldn't afford it—
after taking on a mortgage plus a prayer or two,
we signed the papers, took possession,
claimed that tiny plot of earth as ours,
the first property our family ever owned.

The writer of this psalm makes a different claim:
"The earth is the Lord's and the fulness thereof."
In other words, I may hold legal title to my precious piece
of turf, but ultimately it is not my property,
Lord, but yours. And it's not just the real estate,
terra firma, that is claimed here; everything I own,
everything I'd like to own, everything I am, everything
in all this wide creation is yours, Lord, by right,
and mine only in trust from you.

It can be a liberating moment,
to see oneself a steward, one who holds everything
in trust. If this earth is truly yours, O God, then
I am no longer ultimately and completely responsible for
it all. I do not have to spend my life trying to control,
to corral, to possess everything possible to possess.
I am set free from the obsession with possession,
that bizarre persuasion that the more things I have,
the more alive I am; that the chief purpose of existence
is to pile my heap of property so high that finally
no one can see me, touch me, and I might as well be dead . . .
which is what I soon will be anyway.

Yes, Lord, if you own all of this,
then I can stop my lusting after all the things
I do not have and begin to enjoy the gifts you have
entrusted to my care. Grant me this perspective
as I enter this new day. Let me hold today
in trust from you, and live it for you
to the full, in Christ.

             Amen.

EVENING

This concept, Lord, of stewardship,
of holding all I have in trust from you,
not only frees me from something—this obsession
with possession—it also frees me *for* something—
for the security of sharing.

Something that is mine nowadays
is, by definition, mine and nobody else's.
And in such a world I am always a little afraid
that someday someone will try to take it from me.
But a thing that is shared removes that cause for fear
and creates, instead, this security of sharing.

Not only this,
the less people threaten one another with possessions,
the less they compete with one another for possessions,
the less they have to defend themselves from one another
for possessions, the more they can begin to open up
to one another, can discover one another
in community and fellowship, even friendship,
that rare, rare gift in our times.

We are your most precious gift to each other, Father.
How quickly we forget this in our scramble after things,
gadgets, toys! How eagerly we substitute possessions
for relationships! And then an illness, an accident,
a shotgun in a shopping mall, and we are brought up short,
reminded of what really counts, reminded of the people,
sisters, brothers all, who are more precious
than anything else . . . than any thing else.

Lord God, show me, in this day now past,
how often I have fallen short of this vision
of your family. Work within my life the miracle,
perhaps the only miracle that yet can save me,
even save this troubled, threatened world,
your miracle of love, and love alone.
Amen.

DAY TEN
Psalm 24

MORNING

Even as I begin this new day, Father,
I must realize, if I am at all honest with myself,
that my hands and heart are far from the kind of purity
the psalmist would require here as prerequisite
for entering your presence. He tells me
I must not lift up my soul to what is false,
nor swear deceitfully; then I will receive blessing
from the Lord, vindication from the God of my salvation.

The trouble is that even as I scanned the pages
of this morning's newspaper I felt my soul lift up,
at least a fraction, toward what is false—
those bright ads that promote coveting, the lust
and angry pride, the callousness with which I read
about the suffering of others and then turn the page
so coolly—so that it wasn't just the newsprint
that gave me dirty hands.
So many of these psalms appear to have a strong
self-righteous, moralistic tone about them.
The writers do not hesitate, at times,
to portray themselves as moral paragons who deserve
far better of you, Lord, than they have heretofore received.
They set up what seem to me impossibly high standards
and then claim that they have satisfied them all.

My tradition teaches me to recognize
my own unworthiness, even to affirm it
as the basis for receiving grace through Christ,
my Lord. Yet there can be a falseness in this too,
a kind of hypocrisy in reverse whereby I stress
my own extreme wretchedness in order to qualify
for the completely unmerited grace
you give to sinners.

Teach me, Lord, to strip away all falseness,
all playacting in your holy presence.
Help me to be completely myself,
this self which fails repeatedly
yet still continues striving after goodness.
And accept me, Father, just as I am.
Then show me how I can accept your grace
and in that grace accept myself, and live it
to the full and to your glory.

Amen.

EVENING

Sometimes the words of these old songs
become so familiar through using them in worship
that I forget how strange, how alien,
how almost incomprehensible they really are
to people of my time. All this question-and-answer
fuss about "the King of glory," and gates and doors
being lifted up, at the close of this psalm,
Father, sounds most dramatic; but it deals
with scenes and actions from an age long gone,
gone probably beyond recall.

One thing I must remember, as I study
this, your Word, Lord God, is that its setting
is a highly complex one: much of it was written down
almost three thousand years ago; and therefore
I should not be too surprised if there are
portions which I simply cannot understand. There is
a proper strangeness, an appropriate and realistic distance
between me and many of the tales recounted here.
To assume a miraculous immediacy of communication
between ancient Israel and the twentieth-century U.S.A.
fails to recognize, do justice to the crucial importance
of this Word of yours for its own original time and place.

Teach me to respect the mystery
of this holy book, Lord God. Do not permit me
ever to be satisfied with facile, quick, simplistic
interpretations. Deliver me from my undue haste to relate
everything I read to my own situation, my insistence that
every word be relevant to my personal here-and-now.
Thus may I even come to learn a lesson
from the incomprehensible, to acknowledge
my human limitations, to recognize the vastness,
beyond all of my imagining,
of your eternal being:
that being in which I rest myself this night.
                                        Amen.

DAY ELEVEN
Psalm 42

MORNING

I have always liked this image of the soul,
like a thirsty deer sniffing the air for cool
and crystal streams of living water.
It leads me to imagine my own spirit
wandering the dry and barren wilderness,
yearning for the sweet refreshment of your presence
and your grace, Lord God.

The only trouble with this scene is that,
at least in my experience, the seeking has been
mainly done by you, Father. My part has been to hide,
to avoid, if possible, your searching presence.
It is sad that prayer should have to be a discipline;
that, so often, it takes tough, persistent effort
for me to step aside from all the hectic whirl
of my schedule and seek the peace and solace
to be found in prayer and meditation.

This enormous privilege of being able
to call upon you day and night, this assurance
that you are always more ready to hear than I am
to turn and speak to you, why does it often feel to me
more of a burden than a blessing?
How is it that I can permit the miracle of prayer
to be turned into a daily chore, a grim routine
that has to be performed?

I find something of this same problem
in my family relations, Lord. There too
I find myself reluctant to spend time talking
with the ones I love the most, the folk I really
care about. There's always something else I have to do
more urgently. Familiarity breeds contempt, and perhaps
"family-arity" breeds indifference; or so it seems.
Could it be that, like my loved ones, I believe you are
so readily available that I can always put you off
until a more convenient time?

Then shock me, now, today, with the urgency,
the sheer immediacy of your holy presence, Lord.
That I might know again the terror and
the joy of your salvation.
                    Amen.

EVENING

Memory can be a healing, a renewing gift.
"These things I remember, as I pour out my soul,"
sings the psalmist; and in remembering past days of joy
and jubilation in your presence, Lord, he is renewed
in faith and hope to meet the future.

As I read through these psalms—
through all the Hebrew scriptures—
I find the same process occurring many times
as individuals, or the entire people of Israel
are called to remember all the mighty deeds
you have carried out on their behalf,
the great deliverances with which
you have redeemed them time and again.

I find this to be valid also in my own life, Father.
"Count your blessings" may seem, at times,
a trite and hackneyed sentiment, and yet it works.
When times are difficult, even desperate,
and despair lurks close around the corner,
the past becomes not an escape but a treasury
from which to draw resources for the present.

As I look back and see
how you have brought me safe, thus far;
as I recall the many other testing periods,
hours and days of gray and dreary desolation,
which have ended with a new song on my lips,
a thankful shout of praise for your deliverance;
I am strengthened for the present trial, reassured
that you have not left me alone and never will.

There is a promise hidden in the past,
Lord God. In these quiet evening moments
guide me as I too "pour out my soul" in remembrance
with the psalmist. So shall I rediscover hope
and sing with him:

> Why are you cast down, O my soul,
> and why are you disquieted within me?
> Hope in God; for I shall again praise him,
> my help and my God.

Amen.

DAY TWELVE
Psalm 46

MORNING

As I talk, on occasion, Lord,
with people who have no interest in the church
and no hesitation in telling me so,
I get the feeling that they are waiting for you
to prove yourself, to jump out at them and say "Boo!"
one dark and foggy night. They go about their daily lives—
daily business—as if you do not exist,
because you have not yet given them an exclusive
demonstration of your almighty and inimitable power.
"Now if only I could find some definite proof,
some fully conclusive evidence that God exists,
then certainly I would come back to church,
would pray and read the Bible, change my way of life.
But until that time, farewell!" That's all they ask!

But these psalms would seem to suggest
a different, indeed completely opposite procedure.
"Be still, and know that I am God" demands, in fact,
an absolute reversal in the above order of events.
After all, how can anyone expect to know you
if they are so busy making money, spending money,
having fun, staying fit, keeping up
with all the latest fads and fancies,
that they can never find the time to listen for
and pay attention to your Word?

I read a curious tale recently
about an ancient, dusty city in the land of Israel
in which, so they say, there are pure underground
rivers of water that rush beneath the busy streets.
But it is only after dark, in the stillness,
when those streets are all deserted, that one can
hear their gurgling sound, and realize
that they are really there.

In the quiet of this early morning hour
let me hear the murmur of your strength and power,
the steady flowing of the river whose streams
make glad your holy habitation, Lord.
Then let me rise, refreshed to know your presence
with me throughout this new day.

                            Amen.

EVENING

This word, "Be still . . ."
more than any other, is the word
I need to hear from this psalm, Lord God.

I need to be still with myself;
not always, every moment, busy involving,
improving, educating, advancing, or diverting myself.
I need time to simply be myself and know myself,
my fortes and my failings, my depths and heights,
my goals as yet unrealized, my dreams, some of them now
almost abandoned with the years, the fears that drive me on.
Why, Lord, am I so afraid to be alone
with my own self?

I need to be still with those I love.
When I am home I always seem to find myself
paying the bills, mowing the lawn, fixing the shutters,
reading the papers or the mail, watching the news,
doing anything rather than be still and know,
or at least begin to talk and listen,
learn to know the ones I love.

And I desperately need to be still with you,
Lord God. That's how this faith I claim to hold
is nurtured, after all, and has the chance to grow.
Not by dramatic revelations out of the blue,
at least in my experience, but by quiet acts of love
and contemplation, by this steady daily discipline
of prayer and meditation—even when it seems to be going
nowhere beyond the walls of this my room.

"Take time," I wrote myself one New Year's Day.
"Take time, my friend, for time will soon enough
take you, forever." Lord, please persist in bidding me
to take time, my own time. Remind me, daily, to be still,
as I have been this night. For only thus may I transform
my hurried footsteps into a pilgrimage of faith,
into the pathways of eternity.
                         Amen.

DAY THIRTEEN
Psalm 51

This great song of repentance
is full of familiar verses, phrases,
expressions; familiar not only because
I have heard them again and again in worship
and in prayer, but also because they ring true
in my own life, my own condition, Lord.

For all the rationalizations of this age,
the case studies, explanations, justifications of
so many of the social scientists that have made sin
an outdated, quite outmoded concept, something left over
from those terrible Dark Ages, a phenomenon
that can better be explained by biology, heredity,
environment, and the rest; for all of these
I still know, deep inside, exactly what
this writer means when he prays:

> Create in me a clean heart, O God,
> and put a new and right spirit within me.

Guilt, as I have come to know it,
is no pathological relic but the natural
result of the way I live, and fail to live.
Guilt, in and of itself, is no disease. It is only
when guilt festers unresolved, knows no penitence

and cleansing, no healing grace of your forgiveness,
Lord, that it can destroy a person, eat away,
entire, the human soul.

This song, with all its honesty and
deep contrition, also recognizes what Saint Paul
spelled out, much later, in his Letter to the Romans:
that only you, O God, can cleanse, can restore a person
to a right and true relationship with yourself.
Only you, O Lord, can give me back the joy
in which my faith was born, sustain me
in my daily walk of faith.

Therefore, as I begin another day,
I would borrow now this ancient, faithful,
and familiar prayer to start things right:

> Create in me a clean heart, O God,
> and renew a right spirit within me.

Amen.

EVENING

As I kneel in your presence this night,
Father, I would once again borrow the words
of this psalm to set all that I say into true
and full perspective:

O Lord, open thou my lips,
and my mouth shall show forth thy praise.

So often, Lord, when I am the one who opens
these lips they will do anything but praise you;
and so I bid you now to take control, to shape my phrases,
frame my syllables, form and mold the content
of my communication, so that it may, at least in some way,
reflect you; so that I might show forth
your glory with my life.

You tell me here, Father,
what it is that I must do to please you.
No lavish and impressive sacrifice upon the public altar,
no grim, pale-faced renunciation that will gain me
credit in the popular eye as "such a sincere person,"
but the inner spiritual gift
of brokenness, contrition.

This is a brokenness that yields
itself in order to be mended and reshaped
within the Master's hands; a brokenness that sees
how bread has to be torn apart in order to be shared,
to bring life to all around, enable songs of praise
to rise from lips that all have tasted grace abundant.
This is a brokenness can lead me to a lonely cross
as it did him who offered up the one,
true sacrifice, acceptable to you.

Remind me of his sacrifice this night,
Lord God; bind its meaning deep within my bones
and blood as I sleep; and help me to be worthy
to follow in his footsteps.
Amen.

DAY FOURTEEN
Psalm 84

MORNING

There is something in me, Lord,
that rebels against the kind of adoration
of the House of God I read of in this psalm.
This thirsting, swooning, yearning to be present in
the temple is so alien to me. It was my forebears,
the Protestant Reformers, in their zeal for a simpler,
more spiritual faith, who denounced every effort to render
beautiful or "holy" any one particular place or shrine.

How, then, do I begin to comprehend this genuine devotion:
the intensity of those Jews who surrounded me some years ago
at the Wailing Wall; the profound, almost palpable emotion
of a noonday crowd in Saint Peter's Square; the supreme
and awe-full sacredness that leads the Muslims
to insist that one must leave one's shoes
outside the Dome of the Rock?

Add to all this the ethical dimension,
that concerned, practical voice which argues
all the treasures of the Vatican would best be sold
to feed the poor; and I catch something
of the dilemma inherent in this psalm.

What about the fundamental need for beauty, wonder,
majesty, that drive to dedicate the fruits of creativity

to the Giver of all gifts—a drive that raised
the glorious cathedrals out of human vision, sacrifice,
and hard labor? It is also true the attitudes
of my Puritan ancestors in the faith produced a barrenness,
a bleak poverty in worship, in the sad belief that grim,
austere surroundings clear the mind of distractions,
lead to pure, uncluttered visions of yourself.

This psalm itself knows beauty, bears a grace
within its language that ushers in the reader to the presence
of true holiness and awe. Perhaps the selfsame content
could have been conveyed in plain and ordinary speech,
pedestrian images, but I don't believe it, Lord.
There is that within true beauty, in buildings
or in language, that leads home the soul to you.
Open my eyes to seek that grace in all I meet today.
And when I find it drive me to my knees.

Amen.

EVENING

"How lovely is thy dwelling place, O Lord of hosts!"
I say this graceful line, let it sound across my lips,
resound within my head, take root in my imagination,
and it conjures up no concept, creed, or cause.
I am led, rather, to a place, to the sanctuary,
the church where I grew up—where I was married,
my children were baptized—but to a place, a building,
a spot somewhere that people have made beautiful
because they sensed God's presence there.

Yes, Lord, I realize you are everywhere.
I have felt your presence close beside in hospital rooms
and barrack rooms, courtrooms and classrooms too.
But I also need a shrine, a sanctuary,
somewhere set apart for silence and for song,
for secret longings and common hopes, a room where
I can lose myself and find myself again, a space
where I can bend my knees, bow my head, fold
my hands, then spread my wings in prayer.

I remember Jesus faced the same question
that I find within this psalm, when a woman brought
an alabaster jar of costly ointment to anoint his feet
and folk rebuked her for the waste. Jesus said,

> Let her alone. . . . She has done a beautiful thing to me.
> For you always have the poor with you,
> and whenever you will, you can do good to them;
> but you will not always have me.

Perhaps Jesus is suggesting that my quandary is false,
an exercise in self-deception; my debate between building
lovely shrines and feeding the poor is all too often
an excuse for doing neither when, in actual fact,
I could often do at least my share of both.

Teach me, good Lord, to love your house
and to love with equal devotion your family
of every house and home. Train me, as your doorkeeper,
to make all persons welcome and to fit your house
to welcome them, through Christ who is the host.

Amen.

DAY FIFTEEN
Psalm 90

MORNING

I know this psalm almost as well
as I know the beloved twenty-third, Father.
I hear it read and sung on great occasions.
It has a music of its own, majestic, stately,
elegiac, like some vast and dizzying cathedral
built with the sounds and syllables of speech.

It begins with the everlasting,
that eternal being of yours, Father, which spans
all ages, all beginnings, and all endings with the words:
"From everlasting to everlasting thou art God."
Then, within this ageless context, the song sings
of human finitude and transience. In immortal words
I read here of mortality. In starkly realistic terms
I am challenged to face up to human frailty,
to recognize myself, a fearful, frail, and finite creature
whose days on earth are strictly limited and fleeting.

I find here no easy reassurance of immortality,
no swift and soothing promises of life beyond the grave.
This writer seems devoid of all concern with any
personal survival or salvation. He is content to recognize
his own—and all humanity's—insignificance when seen
in the perspective of eternity. He does not whine or storm
the heavens with complaints. Rather, he glories
in the majesty of your eternal purpose, Lord.

My faith, and that of many I see about me,
is too caught up in the search for personal salvation, Lord.
This splendid, ancient song sets all such petty yearnings,
all subjective individual considerations, within their
proper context, within the awe-filled adoration
of the One who creates life and death, who is
"from everlasting to everlasting."

Help me, Lord God, to see beyond concern
with my own fate; to realize eternal life is not available
on individual personal terms alone; to relocate myself
in the entire community of being, your creation;
and then to live this day, all days, with thanks
as they are given from your hand.

Amen.

EVENING

There is a truth,
this solemn psalm reminds me,
older than death, even older, far, than life.
It is the truth of God: the conviction that,
beyond all common reason, everything that is, has been,
is yet to be is formed and undergirded,
guided far beyond all futures
by that One whose will is good,
whose word is sure, whose very being
has the stamp, the shape, the clear
and full identity of love.

In this is hope.
Not in myself or in humanity,
in science, enterprise, intelligence,
wondrous as these gifts can be at times;
but in you, Lord God, who are
"from everlasting to everlasting."

Having faced the full reality of death,
having found the goal to be not the escape from death,
rather the sanctification of each moment of my life,
this psalmist bids me cling to you
as One who, yet, can fill my fleeting days
with joy and ringing gladness. The message here
is not of gloom and doom, the grim absurdity
of all existence, but of fulfillment in the call
to enjoy such days as are given within the setting
of your own eternal providence and plan.

I would rest me in that providence this night,
secure not in myself but in your being
and your everlastingness. And one thing more:
the trust that, in the full and final ripening
of your providence and grace, this blade of grass
that flourishes and withers now will wave again
within a full and golden field
at harvesttime.
                    Amen.

DAY SIXTEEN
Psalm 100

MORNING

"Make a joyful noise to the Lord, all the lands!"
I've seen so many Christians, so many congregations,
read or sing this psalm in worship, Father.
They sing in such a solemn, dour, and dreary way
that I wonder whether they have ever yet permitted
the rich meaning of these words to percolate beyond
their tight-set lips and reach into their minds.

The psalm talks of joy and gladness—
the old metrical version that I used to sing in Scotland
even said, "Him serve with mirth," and mirth,
as far as I can tell, means merriment and laughter.
The way most Christians sing, the only appropriate laughter
might be a sad, ironic chuckle. Lord, what happened
to rejoicing on its way into the church?

Jesus, as I read about him in the Gospels,
was the antithesis of this killjoy view of faith.
His teachings, even now, after nearly twenty centuries,
communicate a fundamental gladness in his attitude to life.
I'm sure he laughed and sang, and even danced for joy
at times. We sing of him as "Lord of the Dance,"
and yet we chant these lively words
while standing rooted to the spot.
"Dance, then," we cry, "wherever you may be"—

and completely fail to see the foolishness involved,
the sheer hilarity of singing words like these
while moving nothing but our lips.

Jesus' chief opponents were those who turned religion
into a dreary thing of rules and regulations, obligations
that squeezed the juice from life like a steamroller crushing
an orange. Why is it that the church seems to have deserted
the poor orange and climbed aboard the steamroller?

Show me, Lord, in this bright new day,
how to live this joy that permeates my faith,
how to communicate the laughter and the gladness
that lies within this gospel of good news.

        Amen.

EVENING

There is another, deeper, question
that might be asked about this psalm's call to rejoice.
In times like these, with innocent victims
filling the daily headlines, with traditional values,
family structures, endangered species in the land,
with a race war bubbling on the brink in Africa
and worldwide annihilation poised for delivery
just behind the nuclear trigger . . . in times like these,
what is there to rejoice about?
Is not rejoicing a luxury I cannot afford, a blasphemy,
Lord, against your call to feed the hungry, house the poor,
work ceaselessly for justice and for peace?

And there is power in this argument, and truth.
Churches and Christians who ignore it, who spend
all their time in clapping hands and dancing hallelujahs,
may well clap and dance their way right into hell,
the hell of selfish, loveless, empty death.

Might there be another kind of joy, Father, a true
and genuine rejoicing to be found right in the midst of all
the turmoil and the struggles of this world? Is there,
perhaps, a deeper celebration to be discovered,
not in fleeing from distress, not in hiding from the tragedies
that surround, but in the very act of facing trouble,
of challenging despair, of investing and committing life
to the task that Christ my Lord began and calls me to today?

That surely was the secret of his joy, a joy
not of evasion but immersion, of full identification
with this world and its problems. In such immersion
all the honest, deep-down joys of life break through,
break through the depths of pain and wear a smile
that is forever true, forever undefeated.

Teach me to rejoice today, as I follow you, Lord,
through all the crowded ways of life, as I discover you
gone on ahead to blaze the trail of human possibility,
as I join hands with you in healing, mending,
making peace, and building up the kingdom.
                                        Amen.

DAY SEVENTEEN
Psalm 104

MORNING

What a marvelous creation I find,
Lord, in this all-encompassing psalm of wonder.
Its vision spans the entire universe, sun and moon,
darkness and light. Yet, for all this, the song
is also filled with intimate scenes from nature:
the stork building her home in the fir tree,
the sea monster sporting in the ocean deeps,
the young lions roaring for their prey.

There is more here, however,
than a picture, some cosmic diorama
of your infinite creativity. In thus displaying
all your universe, the psalmist is also showing me
a message about that universe, the message that,
in all its rich and bewildering diversity, this cosmos
is your handiwork, Lord, the splendid expression
of your divine imagination.

What I do not find here, Lord,
no matter how hard I search, is a step-by-step,
scientific account of precisely how you carried out
that creation. Yes, it reads in places
like the Creation account in Genesis, but that story too
must surely not be seen as a source which rejects science,
astronomy, physics, and the like. These Bible stories

of creation do not answer my question "How?"
they address the universal question, "Why?"
Surely you never intended this great Book of Books
to be a geology textbook. Your focus is far grander,
far more encompassing than that. When I reduce
these thrilling verses to some treatise on biology
or archaeology, I lose sight of the forest
while examining the trees.

You remind me as I read this psalm, Lord,
that this book, this Bible, is a song, not an equation
or a theorem. As a song it sings a truth that goes beyond
any and all test tubes and laboratories to the most ultimate
of questions: questions about hope and meaning, love
and fear, judgment and grace, darkness and light.

Open my eyes in this new day to the grandeur
that is all about me, Father, and may I recognize there
your shaping hand, your providential care.

Amen.

EVENING

This panoramic psalm, Lord,
sets me in true perspective; perhaps the crown
of your creation, yet still and all, only a part,
one component part of that creation along with the plants
and the wild goats, the mountains and the seas,
the beasts of the forest and the badgers
who find refuge in the rocks.

Nothing, this writer would insist,
nothing in this world is really useless.
Every part of it has purpose for one or another
of God's creatures. This universe was not made simply
for my profit and amusement, let alone my exploitation.
It is to be the home of all your manifold creation,
the scene of your rejoicing in the fundamental
goodness of all things.

And if this message was true, Father,
when this old psalm was written, how much more so
in my time, when not only entire species
are threatened daily with extinction, but
the entirety of life is held hostage
to the pressing of a button in
a presidential briefcase.

This world is your creation.
More than that; this world is your own property,
property you have given to be rejoiced in
as I learn to take my place with all your creatures
and sing my own unique and personal part
within the cosmic hymn of praise.

Deliver me from that poverty of vision,
Lord, that could ever find this world a dull
and dreary place. Teach me to cherish your world
and care for it; to find, both within
and beyond all things, your presence,
your beauty, and your grace.

                              Amen.

DAY EIGHTEEN
Psalm 118

MORNING

> This is the day which the Lord has made;
> let us rejoice and be glad in it.

"This is the day. . . ." How many times,
good times and bad, have I murmured these four words
to myself as I step forth into a new morning,
"This is the day . . ."?

"This is the day I begin kindergarten,
the day I take my finals, graduate from high school:
This is the day." "This is the day I join the service,
the day I receive my degree from college,
the day that I get married: This is the day."
"This is the day I begin my first job, the day
my child is born, the day I hear from the doctor
about those tests, the day I face major surgery,
the day I leave my last job, the day I say goodbye
to someone I have deeply loved: This is the day."

Good times and bad, Lord,
when I have uttered these words—
"This is the day"—with joy and bright anticipation
on my lips or with anxiety and heavy dread
upon my heart. However, here I learn,
in this great psalm of thanksgiving for deliverance,
that there is more to say than just "This is the day";
that this saying, as it is, is incomplete.

"This is the day which the Lord has made."
The day of deliverance, yes, of course.
But in Jesus Christ, your son, my Savior,
is not every day Deliverance Day? May I not arise
to greet each morning, no matter what it seems to hold
of sunlight or of shadow, with this ancient word
of victory and faith upon my lips,
"This is the day which the Lord has made . . ."?

And one thing more—rejoicing.
For the psalmist adds an invitation here:
"Let us rejoice and be glad in it."
Show me this joy, Father, that lies just below
the surface of all things in your redeemed creation.
Then help me claim this day for you
and live it to your glory.
                    Amen.

EVENING

This is a psalm of surprise,
Father; it sings for joy of a triumph
that seems to have been completely unexpected.
There is a note of sheer astonishment hiding
just beneath the surface here that draws me
to this glad, victorious psalm.

I can imagine Jesus singing it
as he arose from death that glorious Easter morn:

> The stone which the builders rejected
> has become the chief cornerstone—

singing of victory as that massive rock,
selected and rolled into place by all the builders
of death and rejection, tumbled away
from the mouth of the tomb, and the light
spilled forth to make pale the dawn.

Here at the close of this day,
Lord God, teach me again the paradoxical lesson
of amazement; the insight, revealed again and again
in this holy old book, that I should somehow
expect to be surprised, that I should not
be astonished by astonishment.

"Amazing grace," John Newton wrote;
yet people sing of it so often, so familiarly
nowadays, that I wonder what amazement can be left.
It is too easy, Lord, after nearly twenty centuries
of preaching, teaching Christ, to take it all for granted,
to forget the utter shock, yes, even scandal,
that the word of resurrection first created,
that salvation through the cross evoked in people.

Guide me to look for truth
in unexpected places. Teach me never to ignore,
or disregard, merely because light never dawned before in
such a place, through such a person. Continue to surprise
me with your grace just when I least expect it.
Thus may my life become a never-ending
journey of discovery.
                    Amen.

DAY NINETEEN
Psalm 121

MORNING

This psalm opens with a question, Father,
one of the most basic questions: Where can I get help?
I hear this question echoing throughout this book;
throughout this modern, complex, and confusing world;
Who or what can aid me, can assist me to survive
the problems and the pressures that surround?

Some would tell me I must help myself.
This is, after all, the era of "self-help"
with all kinds of books and tapes and programs
to help me get my body, spirit, mind,
my personality, career, relationships, or life in shape.
And they do say that even you "help those
who help themselves." Trouble is, too many of those
who set out to help themselves seem to end up
doing so at other selves' expense.

Yet I believe you do call me to take charge
of my own life, problems and all. You gave me
a mind to think things through, a will to act upon
these thoughts. That Parable of the Talents Jesus told
was surely a stern warning that when you give gifts
you expect them to be used. And as I read this Bible
it is clear that those who call on you for help
do get that help, but it usually arrives in the form

of renewed strength to carry on, to carry through,
rather than escape from all their troubles.

Another way you help, Lord, is through community,
through family, neighbors, church, and wider networks.
The Hebrew prophets called consistently for the protection
and the welfare of the widow, the orphan, and the stranger.
The infant Christian church was urgently concerned
about the needy in their midst. When I cry to you for help,
therefore, I must expect one of the ways you will respond
is through family, church, community, and state.

Open my eyes this day to all the help
I have received, am still receiving, Lord,
through the social structures, bonds, and family ties
that have supported me from birth. Teach me to
recognize and gratefully affirm your providential hand
in all of these. Then let me grasp that hand
and venture forth in trust.
Amen.

EVENING

I often hear this psalm read at funerals, Lord.
And when I hear I sometimes think,
How wrong this is, how irrational! This person died
of cancer, or of heart disease, left behind
a grieving family, an uncompleted life,
while this minister is reciting
"He who keeps you will not slumber" and so forth.
How untrue it is. How absurd!
Then I come again to that wonderful final verse,

> The Lord will keep your going out
> and your coming in from this time forth
> and for evermore.

My going out and my coming in. . . .
My going out in the morning and my coming in
in the evening; my going out to school
and my coming home from college;
my going out to work, to wrestle for a living
in this world, my coming in to food and fellowship,
all the trials and joys of family and home;
my going out to discover, to explore and create,
my coming in to rest, to reflect, to renew;
my going out to the uncertain, the unknown,
my coming in to the One who has known me
since the dawn of time and place and personality;
my going out into the valley of the shadow,
my coming in to a table blessed with
never-ending hospitality.

The Lord will keep my going out,
my coming in . . . forevermore. So that even
my last going out is also followed by a coming in.
In this trust I can know whence my help comes.
In this faith I can look beyond the hills
to glimpse the horizons of your never-failing grace,
the sunrise of your eternal welcome home.

So let me rest in confidence this night.
Amen.

DAY TWENTY
Psalm 122

MORNING

I was glad when they said to me,
"Let us go to the house of the Lord!"

I recite these words to myself, Lord,
and as they ring within my brain, resound back
into my memory, they conjure up scenes there,
scenes from the past which somehow hold
and can evoke again that gladness, that true joy,
which never seems far from the lips
of the writer of these songs.

I see myself, one January morning, Father,
high on the Mount of Olives overlooking old Jerusalem.
We were a travel group of tough, hard-bitten clergy
who had seen it all and then preached most of it.
Yet after a week of touring in the Holy Land
we had become a friendly, rather open crew who could
exchange ideas, swap jokes, without those stiff,
defensive shields so many ministers feel compelled
to wear much of the time.

We climbed down from our familiar touring coach
only to be besieged by the eternal throng of traders
offering all kinds of unbelievable relics
at even more unbelievable prices.
Gradually we fought our way to the edge and looked across

the valley to the fabled city spread out there.
We gazed in sudden silence.
Then someone just behind me began to sing,
"Jerusalem, Jerusalem, lift up your voice and sing.
Hosanna in the highest, Hosanna to the King."
And as others from our group joined in, I scanned
the walls, the gates, the towers, the tombs,
that glorious golden dome—and something deep inside
rejoiced and was exceeding glad. And when I looked around,
there was not one dry eye in all that hardened group
of professional holy men and women.

Yes, Father, there is a joy, a gladness
far beyond description, in that consciousness of standing
before your holy house, the city of our God and King.
Let that gladness walk with me today so that
wherever my path may lead I may still stand
within your gates, Lord, and rejoice.

Amen.

EVENING

Another scene comes to my mind tonight, Lord,
as I reread this psalm of joy; another Holy Land—
at least for Presbyterians. It is Scotland,
Sunday morning, some thirty years ago.

The bells have just begun—there goes the Free Kirk,
then Saint David's, the Auld Kirk, and Saint John's.
Soon footsteps echo on the quiet streets. I see myself,
dressed in my best, indeed, my only suit.
Shoes shining bright. Clean white handkerchief
in top pocket. Bible in hand, offering envelope tucked
safe inside. Up the steps, past the tombstones in the yard,
and through the great high doors to the vestibule
where the elders are handing out the hymnals.

Then on into that great and lofty, solemn room,
the organ playing, the windows filtering warmth and color
into the chilly northern light, the strong oak pews,
table and pulpit, flowers and Sunday hats, the entry
of the choir, and then the beadle with the Bible
leading in the minister himself.
And "Let us worship God" begins the sacred hour
with the singing of a metrical psalm.

> I was glad when they said to me,
> "Let us go to the house of the Lord!"

There was something vast and measureless about
that Sabbath day. Time seemed to move more spaciously
than it did on all the rest. There was something ceremonial
about the clothes we wore, the paths we walked, even the food
we ate that day of days that set it quite aside from all
the other six, that made it really The Lord's Day.
I don't remember ever being forced to go to church.
Maybe I was lucky—I was certainly not all that pious—
but we were glad, truly glad, when Sunday rolled around.
No one even had to say, "Let us go to the house of the Lord."
Where else would anyone go? That's what this day was for!

Father God, I thank you for rich memories.
More than this, I thank you for the gift of gladness
in your presence, the assurance that, wherever I may go,

whatever circumstances I may know, your house awaits
with open door and light within. Even so, lighten my darkness,
Lord, with your radiant presence here tonight.

Amen.

DAY TWENTY-ONE
Psalm 124

MORNING

I am concerned about your neutrality, Lord.
Over the years I had just about concluded that
you are the One who does not take sides, who refuses
to enter into our petty disputes between Right and Left,
East and West, Catholic and Protestant, our side and theirs.
I had convinced myself that you, as the One God of all,
remain supremely above such childish squabbles,
calling your family to the unity and peace
for which you created us.

Now, in today's psalm, I am told
that you are certainly not neutral.

  If it had not been the Lord
  who was on our side,
  let Israel now say—

God on our side? This whole idea troubles me, Father.
So many times throughout history, peoples, nations,
tribes have claimed that you were with them,
have claimed to be your chosen ones, and then used
that claim to justify the most inhuman treatment
of others who were not. And yet this psalm
clearly implies you are not always neutral.

One lesson I might learn here
is that you are not necessarily always on my side.
Oh, yes, ultimately, in the most decisive questions
of life or death, salvation or damnation, you have shown
that you are for me. You proved that once, for all,
on that hill called Calvary, Lord.
But in the everyday opinions I express, the parties
I belong to, causes I espouse, you may be either
for me or against. You could even be—probably are
at this very moment—both for me and against me, depending
on just what I have in mind, and when, and to whom.

My Father God, stay by my side this day
even though you will not always remain on my side.
Hold me firm within your strong, redeeming grace
and help me grow in faith so that, in all I do and say,
I am more closely and more often on your side.

Amen.

EVENING

Whose side are you on, Lord?
Do you remain above the issues,
on a higher sphere somewhere, uninvolved in
the concerns and the crises that divide this world?
Or are you, perhaps, only concerned with personal morality,
all the individual dos and don'ts, like honesty,
fidelity, clean living?

These scriptures, however, suggest a different
attitude. The histories, the prophets, and the Gospels
all portray you as a God who passionately cares
about society and human welfare, about peace
and justice, equality and basic dignity.
Perhaps I must conclude that because you are on "our side"—
all of our sides—you cannot therefore always be
on my individual, personal side. For one thing,
you do not always define the issues as I do.
For another, you will never define enemies
in the same way that I do.

These scriptures also are a guide
for discovering where you stand, just whose side
you may belong to on this issue or the next, Lord God.
They suggest to me that, when in doubt,
I should look for you on the side of the weak
and the oppressed. This does not always tell me
precisely how to vote and who to vote for.
But it does sort out priorities.
It does make clear the goals to be sought after,
and the methods that may be used to reach those goals.

Your Son showed us this way as he
lived out his days among the helpless poor,
as he refused to offer any compromise to power,
as he declined, firmly but politely, to place programs
before persons, to make strategic bargains
which might require the sacrifice
of individual lives.

Grant me the faith and courage, Lord,
to support the poor and the defenseless ones,
even to join you at their side in times of trial.

And to discover in their company that you are truly
on our side, to deliver all your foolish children
from death now and forever.
Amen.

DAY TWENTY-TWO

Psalm 126

MORNING

> Then our mouth was filled with laughter,
> and our tongue with shouts of joy.

There have been moments like that, Lord,
in my life; moments when my entire being has been
swept, caught up, possessed by sheer, clear happiness
and contentment. Holding my child close within my arms.
Magical Christmas mornings in my own early childhood.
Sunrise from a boat out on the bay, the early morning ocean
a vast incandescent mirror to the dawning glory of the sky,
while I float with the tide, transfixed between the two.

Yet such moments are few and far between.
I lose that thrill so quickly, Father, get caught up
instead in all the duties, what I call the "musts" of life.
This world I live in appears tyrannized by the "musts"
of the alarm watch, the buzzer, the beeper.
Everywhere schedules and timetables rule the roost.
Everyone and everything about me, in a land that claims
to cherish human freedom, appears driven and compulsive,
dominated by the mighty gods of duty, obligation,
and necessity, this joyless cult of "must."

In my religion too, Lord God,
people are always telling me exactly what
I *must* do to be saved. I must believe exactly this,

not that, be baptized, attend church and prayer meeting,
read the Good Book and pray each day, give as much
and more than I can, teach Sunday school, and then,
depending on which brand I have in mind, speak in tongues,
write regularly in protest to Washington D.C., support
foreign missions, and smile all the while for Jesus.
And this is not to mention all the things I must not do.

I realize, Father, that most of these
are worthy options for a Christian, fine ways
to give expression to the faith, but are they all
requirements, essential to the process of salvation?
Help me to distinguish what I must from what I may,
Lord God, and thus restore to me, this day,
the joy of thy salvation.
Amen.

EVENING

So much of the life Jesus spoke of, Father,
was based on may, not must. Your Word, in him,
of grace, redemption, deliverance given freely
for the asking and receiving, seems to me to put an end
to "must," to call a halt to all that soul-destroying
business of earning one's own way to heaven
by the meeting of demands.

Correct me if I am wrong, Father,
but, as I understand the Gospels, you offer me,
without prior conditions, life, forgiveness, freedom,
love, a clean, fresh start, support along the way,
and all I *have* to do is to accept it.

After that there are a thousand and one things
that I *may*—not must but may—do. Your gift of life
has set me free to choose to give that life
to those who need my care, my time,
the sharing of my talents. Your gift of joy offers me
the opportunity to praise and celebrate, worship and adore,
not just in church but with every breath I take.
Your gift of love makes possible the privilege
of finding life in losing it, as Jesus did,
for me, for all. This surely is the spring that drives
the Christian: not grim and dutiful obedience
but simple gratitude, the free spontaneous response
to all your gifts.

> When the Lord restored the fortunes of Zion,
> we were like those who dream.
> Then our mouth was filled with laughter,
> and our tongue with shouts of joy.

Show me now, Father, how I can catch this joy
and share it. Not any empty, foolish optimism,
the kind of plastic smiles that people seem to paste on
for TV, but a deep, continuing gladness that reaches out
into the darkest places of this world and lightens
them with love, brightens them with hope.

Amen.

DAY TWENTY-THREE

Psalm 127

MORNING

> Unless the Lord builds the house,
> those who build it labor in vain.

So much of the labor I see in the world
is what this psalmist would call "Labor in vain."
People spend most of their lives, they "earn their living,"
as they put it, in ways that seem far removed
from anything you might be building, Father.

There are so many occupations
in which the only possible motivation
is a financial one, in which the only human goal
can be to have to work no more, to reach quitting time,
the weekend, vacation, or retirement. There are so many
of your children, Lord, who would be only too happy
to labor in vain, to have any kind of labor at all.

This "work" with which we occupy our time
can be, in point of fact, both blessing and curse.
There is, at best, something intensely satisfying about it,
something challenging, fulfilling an essential need within
the human spirit. You labored, after all, Lord God,
at the Creation; even took time off—the seventh day—
to step back and admire all you had made, and call it
"very good." Then you gave the man and woman work to do,
to "have dominion" over all, to "till" and "keep" the garden.

On the other hand, work can become destructive,
not only when it is a fruitless or degrading task
but also when its role expands to dominate a life, when work
becomes obsessive, a demon that drives everything before it,
or an escape from the more challenging demands
of family, relationships, responsibilities.

Guide me to find, in the work I do
this day, Lord God, that blessing which redeems
all tasks from drudgery—your presence by my side.
Give me the strength to keep myself from everything
that works against your kingdom and your will.
Let me taste the joy of being your co-worker
in the building of a world of peace,
of justice, and of freedom.

Amen.

EVENING

As my mind and body wind down
toward the night and rest, Father,
I find within your Word a clear reminder
that dark as well as light is a gift
from your providing hand.

The psalmist helps me take a good long look
at all my "anxious toil," my burning the candle
at both ends in order to achieve, to make a name
for myself, to be successful in the eyes
of those around me. He points me once again
toward the truest, fullest blessings,
those of family and heritage.
He tells me that the proper way to "make a name,"
the way of patriarchs and kings of old,
is by establishing a house, a family built
on firm and sure foundations.

As I remember in my prayers now
those closest to my heart, my wife and children,
parents, brothers, sisters, all the members
of my "household," I realize how often,
in the heat of the long day,
I lose touch with this reality.
I confess that so much of my time is spent
concerned and worried over lesser issues, problems,
plans, priorities which, if I was ever to try
to measure them over against my family,
would fade to insignificance.

Yet I permit such minor details
to dominate and keep me from the ones
who matter most, those without whom my life
would be an empty, lonely desert.

As I take this moment now to raise again
these fond, familiar faces to my mind's eye,
and then to bear them up in prayer before your mercy seat,
bless me through this recognition of my many blessings
And grant to me, as you promise in this psalm
to your beloved, the gift of restful sleep.

Amen.

DAY TWENTY-FOUR
Psalm 130

MORNING

This psalm, Lord, has been classified as
"A Song of Ascents." And as I read it through
I realize how accurate that title is; for it begins
in the abyss and moves steadily toward the heights,
the heights of faith and trust in you.

What, then, are these depths
that call forth such an aching, longing cry?
"Out of the depths I cry to thee, O Lord!"
There are so many deeps that threaten to engulf:
depths of depression or oppression, of illness or poverty,
injustice or bereavement. There is the abyss
of a broken home, with love long gone, dreams and plans
all shattered, bewildered, frightened children, and anger,
hurt, resentment, dominating everything and everyone.
There is the dread chasm of broken health,
that chill hand that grasps and then will not let go,
wishing and not wishing for the phone to ring,
the hospital to call with the test results
that could mean hope or bleak despair.

This cry comes from the dark pit of addiction,
from the deep of mental illness and confusion. It arises
from the knifing, often necessary hurt of teen rebellion,
independence, self-assertion; from the desperate fear

of not making the grade in a society where the grade is
all-important; from the loss of work, the loss of
self-respect, the loss of friendship, the loss of love.

"Out of the depths," Lord,
is a cry, a prayer that rises from so many
in this world, a world which seems all tangled
in a net of its own making, a net of violence and terror,
of lies and deception, of starvation and crushing poverty,
of ignorance, fear, inequity, and prejudice.

Father, let me hear the cry this day.
Do not let me shut it out as I have learned to do
so well. Teach me to listen with your ears to the voice
of your captive children and then to answer
with your love, through Christ my Lord.

Amen.

EVENING

The way out of the depths is the way
of forgiveness, or so this psalm would suggest
to me, Father. I read here that not by any effort
of my own, any form of self-help, or self-assertion,
self-protection, self-elevation, can I climb
out of the depths, but through your forgiveness,
your grace, your everlasting mercy, which provides
a path by which to ascend from the dark abyss.

This forgiveness is difficult to give
and even harder to receive. And yet, after centuries
of retaliation, of tit-for-tat, eye-for-eye,
tooth-for-tooth, which has only brought this world
to the brink of total annihilation, perhaps it is time
to take another, longer look at forgiveness.

If I am to forgive, then I must recognize
not just the evil in the other person: my spouse,
rival, adversary—that is usually not difficult to do.
Forgiveness also demands I recognize the evil in myself,
and on that basis begin to talk, that's all.
No immediate reconciliation—that would surely be
too cheap. Just a basic recognition that both sides
are wrong in part; both sides are sinful, selfish children
of one God. In other words, forgiveness means that I,
that all your children, need to recognize our common
human need of your forgiveness; our universal failure
to live up to what you have created us to be.
Only then, and covered by your grace,
can we turn, at last, and forgive one another.

Might it be, Lord God, that it is only when
we realize that we are all to blame, each and every
blessed one of us, that we, your children, will ever
be able to work together to create a peaceful life,
a peaceful home, a safe and peaceful world?

For all the ways that I have failed, this day,
to recognize my own complicity in the brokenness
of this world, Lord God, I beg for your forgiveness,
now, before I sleep; and for your mercy
to protect me till I wake.
                    Amen.

DAY TWENTY-FIVE

Psalm 130

MORNING

Waiting is not something to which I take kindly.
"Immediately, if not sooner" is the typical demand
of these times I live in, times of instant everything:
instant action, instant results, instant gratification,
even instant love, which some call "instimacy."
The psalmist bids me "wait and hope,"
but I seem to have lost the patience, Lord, for waiting.

I wonder what he means by "wait and hope."
Is this a passive thing in which I put on my clean
white robe and climb the nearest mountaintop to attend
the Second Coming of your Son? Or might there be an active
kind of waiting, a dynamic sense of trust, a powerful
focusing of all my being upon you, Lord, an expectancy
which, even in anticipation, sets up quite new priorities,
redirects whatever else I do, or do not do?

To live in waiting upon you would not, then,
have to be a tedious, weary, dragged-out
waiting-room existence. Rather it could partake of
the lively, vibrant anticipation of expectant parents
or the barely suppressed excitement of children
just before the dawn of Christmas Day.

The eager longing in this song—
with its twice-repeated

   more than watchmen for the morning—

should set my life on tiptoe as I enter
into this new day. The morning, after all, has come.
My watch, my eager longing, must be even closer
to fulfillment than the psalmist's long ago.
Even so, come, Lord Jesus, and claim this day,
and claim this life to be your own.
                              Amen.

EVENING

The heights of hope, that's where this psalm
concludes, high lifted up upon the lofty certainty
of your redemption, Lord my God.

> For with the Lord there is steadfast love,
> and with him is plenteous redemption.
> And he will redeem Israel from all his iniquities.

Father, this world appears so unredeemed at times.
Despite almost two thousand years of preaching, praying,
witnessing, the news headlines, the city streets,
the corners of my mind and of my life seem to belong
much more beside the cross than by the empty tomb.
The betrayal and brutality go on and on,
and cries "out of the depths" sound more familiar
to my ears than any victor's shout of triumph.

This very day that I am rounding out in prayer
has known too much of self-deceit, of faithlessness,
defeat, and even moments of despair. My faith in you
feels fledgling, at the very best; unable to progress
beyond that infants' milk Paul wrote of
to the solid food—adult life in Christ.

Help me to catch the signs and signals
that the psalmist caught; to glimpse in acts of mercy—
those solitary yet innumerable deeds of kindness, trust,
self-sacrifice—the workings of your Spirit. Lift my soul
through all the glories of this natural creation,
sunrise and sunset, forest and mountain, springtime, fall.
Grant me that vision by which your prophets could pierce
beyond the chaos and confusion to a day that will be
your day, Lord, a day of justice and of mercy,
a day of victory that is already won
and waiting to be claimed.

Thus let me "wait for the Lord" in hope and trust.
Teach me to live victoriously in the here-and-now.
And so begin to move, not just myself, but this whole world,
this vast and eagerly awaiting universe,
out of the depths and into the kingdom
of your Son, my Savior, Jesus Christ.

Amen.

DAY TWENTY-SIX

Psalm 131

MORNING

I love this psalm, Lord, because of its simplicity
and its humility. So many of these songs of the spirit
soar with grand poetic eloquence, with magnificent
descriptions, with high resounding phrases.
I feel challenged by them, inspired at times
but also, sometimes, just a bit left out.
My life is hardly ever as dramatic, as exciting,
as these psalms. This little song of serenity and calm
tells me that I belong here too, that even though the great
and marvelous play no part in my days, I am your child;
you nurture me like a mother with her infant at her breast.

What a daring image here, Lord God!
This writer-singer pictures you, not as a lofty monarch,
majestic ruler of the stars of heaven, the cosmos,
but as a mother, gentle with her baby,
performing that first basic, essential, and life-giving task,
the selfless sharing of her strength in loving tenderness.

I need to keep this scene within my mind
to balance all the other metaphors I find of you
as angry judge, even as jealous tyrant. Indeed, this scene
belongs, for me, beside that other one of you as father
running forth to greet your lost, rebellious son,
with tears of joy, embraces full of welcome.

I need to know you also as "my heavenly mother";
to bring within my thinking and my feeling about you
all of those emotions and experiences I have cherished
from my earliest days of being mothered with such tender
and devoted kindly care. You have been, still are, a mother
to me, God, and as I recall my own mother my faith expands,
my hope grows even surer, my love for you grows
ever deeper, more filled with thankfulness.

I rejoice this morning, realizing that,
beyond all names and titles—Lord and King, Redeemer,
Shepherd, even Father, Mother—you are Love. Help me
to recognize your presence in this day wherever love
is to be found and, when I find it, to be glad
that I belong within your family of grace.

Amen.

EVENING

As I reread this gentle psalm
of trust and deep assurance, I am held
within the circle of your grace, the warm embrace
of your abiding faithfulness.

This picture of a child held at its mother's breast
sets new horizons to my view of life in faith,
lends new meaning to that saying of your Son
that we must be as little children in your kingdom.

Adulthood, maturity, in twentieth-century terms
is all tied up with independence. We see freedom,
nowadays, as a state in which we need depend on no one,
in which we are fully capable of taking care of ourselves.
But this world in which you set us,
these societies we participate in, do not permit
this kind of rugged individualism.
Whether we like it or not,
you have bound us all together within the web of life,
and cooperation, not competition, is the true secret
of the game, the one requirement
if we are ever to survive and move ahead.

Might it be, Lord God, that true maturity
is to realize precisely our dependence upon you
and one another? Could the full expression of our freedom
be to freely choose to join the human family, to share
its tasks and challenges, to bind ourselves in love
into the chain of human suffering and hope?

This psalm's powerful portrayal of a mother
and her child tells me that until I can admit the fact
of my total dependence upon you, then all my independence
is a sham, a childish make-believe which keeps me
from the way, the truth, the life.

Hold me to yourself this night,
my Mother God, and nourish me through the dark hours
with the milk of divine tenderness and peace.

                                               Amen.

DAY TWENTY-SEVEN
Psalm 133

MORNING

From time to time I run across an image
in this book that seems completely alien,
an expression that simply fails to come across.
One example is right here in this psalm,
where the writer speaks with satisfaction and delight
of precious oil poured over someone's head,
running down the hair and beard,
dripping onto the collar of his robes.
Such an experience holds little attraction for me, Lord—
for most of us in this squeaky-clean culture we call "home."
But the message that this image celebrates, the blessedness
of brothers and sisters when they dwell in unity together,
this is a universal concept, a universal dream.

Yet does this psalm itself not point up a major problem?
For as long as peoples are so radically different, as long
as some count oil on their clothes a sign of blessing,
while others see it only as a mess, what hope is there
for any kind of unity among such diverse creatures?

This world of yours, of ours, Lord God,
is filled with different customs, divergent value systems,
ways of life. If unity was your original idea, Father,
then things surely went wrong somewhere along the way.
Yet unity need not mean uniformity. People with all kinds

of different backgrounds, customs, preferences,
can come together, work together, when they share
a common purpose. I see this not only in the church
but in politics, in business, in the United Nations.
It seems that folk when facing a common threat,
or attracted by a common goal, can submerge differences,
ignore those things on which they disagree,
and find at least a temporary unity.

Make this blessed unity a goal within my days, Lord God.
Help me discover the great things that bind us all together,
all your children; then let me appreciate and learn from
all the lesser things, the local things, those habits
and traditions that lend color to the human race.
Let me taste the joy of all our rich diversity,
yet also recognize and work toward that unity
that sparkles up ahead like the dew upon Mount Hermon.

Amen.

EVENING

I read this psalm of unity tonight
against the background of a still-divided world.
"Resurgent nationalism" is a code word in the headlines.
Wars and pseudo-wars rage on for years between
brothers and sisters in the faith—different kinds
of Muslim mow each other down in the Middle East,
different kinds of Christian blow each other up in Ireland.

Yet in my personal life, Father,
I have seen tremendous progress over the years.
At least since good Pope John XXIII we Protestants
and Catholics have learned, first to respect and then
to love each other just a bit. We have even managed,
here and there, to worship you in the same place,
at the same time; and this had never happened
in the past four hundred years of division and suspicion.

We Christians and Jews, appalled at all the horror
wrought by centuries of ignorance and cruel prejudice,
have begun to draw together too, to worship on occasion,
to study one another's ways and customs, to pray
and read the scriptures, to come to know and even care
for one another as fellow children of the Book with
much we hold in common, as well as much that still divides.

People nowadays do not realize, Father,
just how amazing this is, how unprecedented
in the history of faith are all these friendly
local links between different families of your children.
The warfare and the hatred are not all that surprising,
given the dismal record of our past. What is surprising,
revolutionary, and refreshing is that, at last,
after three thousand years and more, the teaching
of this psalm is being heard and even lived
for the first time on so wide and warm a basis.

Father, I thank you for great leaders like Pope John,
who have called your church to unity once more, and for
all those brave, persistent souls who have insisted
on living out the blessedness you have promised
when sisters and brothers dwell in unity.

Amen.

DAY TWENTY-EIGHT

Psalm 137

MORNING

This song of rare and solemn beauty,
this gem of human craft and loveliness,
speaks to me this morning, Lord, as it has spoken
to age after age, of that universal sense of longing,
exile . . . homesickness. And the first miracle
lies, for me, Lord God, in this:
that anyone could create such a poem in the setting
of the prison camps of Babylon.
This poet was a hostage, I remind myself,
one of that vast throng of captives dragged off
in chains to Babylon when that mighty empire conquered
Judah and Jerusalem. Yet amid all the turmoil, torment,
persecution, as his captors "required of him a song"
he could not forget his homeland, the city of his God.
And in immortal lines he sings of his devotion
and his longing for
"Jerusalem above my highest joy!"

But then the mood abruptly changes.
This lovely wistful melody is suddenly transformed
into a hymn of angry hate as the singer calls down judgment
and destruction, curses Babylon, and cries:

Happy shall he be who takes your little ones
and dashes them against the rock!

From the sublime to the obscene;
from the universal longing to be home again
to the taking of tiny infants and beating out their brains.
All in one song! Lord, what kind of creatures are we?
What kind of paradox, of grandeur and of misery,
of Hitler and of Beethoven, Genghis Khan and Leonardo,
makes up our human frame? Am I, at heart, a contradiction,
a living antithesis, a walking chaos, beauty and the beast?

Grant me the honesty, Father, to face
both the sublime and the obscene; to recognize
their reality in my world and in myself. Then to offer
myself up to you in faith that you can turn my chaos
into order, my paradox to single-minded service
in your name and to your glory.

                    Amen.

EVENING

There is one who knows this paradox—
the grandeur and the misery of humankind—
knows it most intimately and profoundly because
he lived it as no other ever has.
In your Son, Jesus Christ, Lord God, I see
the greatness and the wretchedness, the grandeur
and the misery brought together, yet without the hate,
without the malice, without the burning for revenge.
In his life and death the heights of love,
your love, reached down, embraced the depths
of human sin and pride and violence.
He embraced it, took it to himself, and thus removed
its sting, defused the bomb, cut through the deadly chain
of violence-returned-for-violence that has held
humanity locked tight within its grasp
from the earliest dawn of time.

Since that day the door has been wide open,
the way has been made clear, the secret of your entire
creation has been uncovered, the secret of your love.
Love is the way, the only way to life,
and the longer I neglect it, the longer I will weep
for a land that is my home even though I never knew it,
never trod its soil or breathed its air.

That is the longing that yearns within the heart
of all your people, Lord: the longing for love,
the promise up ahead of a land and of a time
when your children will breathe free, will eat well,
will grow strong, will know love.
This is the challenge that redeems my life
from emptiness and sets my days within the context
of eternity. So let me rest this night within
that bright eternal context, your grace
in Jesus Christ my Lord.
                    Amen.

DAY TWENTY-NINE

Psalm 139

MORNING

Nowadays this psalm would probably
be written in the opposite direction:
"O Lord, I have searched you and known you!"

Everything today seems to center
around the great almighty I. This is
an egocentric world, not a theocentric one;
a world where no one would even think of questioning
the assumption that any searching that is done
is done from this side of the equation,
is carried out by humankind in search of you,
Lord God, and not the other way around.

Yet when this search begins with me,
when I initiate the process, Lord, the results
are altogether different. Whenever human beings
sit down behind a yellow pad, a clay tablet, or even
a computer and seek, through the exercise of reason alone,
to figure out what you, God, must be like—what a god,
simply in order to be God, should, at a minimum, comprise—
the result is always less than personal.
We tend to finish up with lists of attributes,
with lengthy and enormously qualified definitions,
with all those ponderous "omnis"—
omniscient, omnipresent, omnipotent—but never

with a person, a dynamic, passionate, personal being
like this Father God I meet in prayer.

Could it be that theologians need
to pray much more and write much less?
Is this the secret of this book of psalms,
that it speaks in prayers and not in propositions?

Search me this day, Lord God,
make clean whatever fails to meet your gaze,
and find in me, through grace, a servant fit
to labor in your vineyard.
                    Amen.

EVENING

This psalm suggests to me
that it is more important to be known by you,
than to know you, Lord my God. All I really need
to know is that I am known in all the deepest
Hebrew connotations of that verb "to know,"
which implies not merely mental knowledge
but a complete and intimate personal relationship:
that of a friend, a family member, lover.

To know that someone knows my name,
my inner self, my dreams, my nightmares,
my desires, my aspirations can be either
a reassuring or a terrifying piece of information.
So much depends on the identity of the knower.

To know that you, the Father of whom
Jesus taught, the Creator and Redeemer
whose providence and care shone through in
every moment of his life and ministry, even his death
and resurrection, the Judge whose justice wears
the flowing robes of loving-kindness—
to know that you know me and are concerned
with every moment, every word, and every thought
is a knowledge that is almost "too wonderful for me":
a knowledge which I find profoundly comforting.

The psalmist asks, in words of flowing eloquence,
where he might flee from your eternal presence, Lord.
Yet that flight becomes a voyage of discovery for the soul
as he finds, even beyond the limits of his thought
and rich imagination, your strong, supporting hand,
your Spirit to uphold and guide.

Even so, this night, wherever in thought or dreams,
worries or wild anticipations I might wander,
be there with me, Father, watching over me,
preserving me from evil, and leading me
"in the way everlasting."
                              Amen.

DAY THIRTY
Psalm 150

MORNING

This note of praise runs all throughout
these psalms like a ground swell underlying
every mood, so that, time and again, from the depths
of despair, the heat of righteous indignation,
or the pain of dreadful torment, a song of praise
will suddenly break through like rays of sunlight
piercing layers of dark and heavy cloud.

And yet the praise of God
has often seemed to me a futile effort,
if not a suspect one. How can I hope to find
words that are fitting to sing your glory, Lord?
It's almost like an ant trying to glorify Mount Everest.
No utterance of mine can even begin to point toward
the majesty and mystery in which you dwell, O God.

And even if I could appropriately praise,
the act would strike me still as dangerously close
to flattery, ingratiation, a questionable attempt
to work my way into your good books, Lord.
I am reminded of those servile courtiers of the past,
who sought advancement, influence, royal favor,
by the lavish application of bootlicking.
How can I sing your glory and yet abandon all self-interest?

Perhaps the first answer I must hear is that
I cannot do so. All my feeble attempts at praise
seem predestined to fall flat upon their faces,
which is probably where they belonged in the first place.
Could it be, then, that true praise begins
in humble and attentive silence?

To hold my peace.
To be completely still and wait upon you.
To listen to the world, the air, the living beings about me.
To sense myself, once again, a part of something vaster,
far lovelier, more harmonious, more mysterious
than humanity can ever be alone. To find myself
belonging to and caught up in an entire living, praising
creation. This must be, at the very least, the birth
of praise—to be still and in that stillness
know that you are God.

Amen.

EVENING

Praise, which begins in silence,
does not always have to end there, Lord.
It may continue in the spontaneous,
almost involuntary response to the secret
I discover in the silence: the secret
of your grandeur and your grace.

Far from any contrived or conniving attempt
at winning favor, gaining influence in your sight,
true praise flows to my lips just as naturally,
as instinctively, as my hands leap to applaud
after a masterly performance, just as naturally as
I turn to one I love, while witnessing a splendid sunset,
and whisper, "Isn't this glorious!"

Not to praise you, Lord my God, would be like
standing on the rim of the Grand Canyon without
even saying, "Ah!" It would be like receiving
the greatest gift of all, the complete gift of trusting,
open love, and then forgetting to say "Thank you,"
neglecting to respond with an "I love you" in return.
When I enjoy something I praise it. It is only human nature
to want to turn to someone and exclaim,
"How wonderful this is! How simply marvelous!"

So too with you, Lord God.
You demand from your children
no cringing, grudging acts of routine praise.
You invite us to enjoy you, to discover you in every moment,
bright or shadowed, and then to join the song of gladness
which is the hymn of all creation, turning,
and returning to its source.

Lord, make of me an Alleluia.
Let my whole being form one high, resounding shout,
combining gratitude and wonder in a lifelong
exclamation point of never-ending praise.

Amen.